THE CATCHER IN THE RYE

NOTES

including
- *Biographical Note*
- *Introduction to the Novel*
- *General Plot Summary*
- *List of Characters*
- *Chapter Summaries and Commentaries*
- *The Holden-Salinger Canon*
- *Questions for Review*
- *Suggested Theme Topics*

by
Robert B. Kaplan, Ph.D.
University of Southern California

INCORPORATED

LINCOLN, NEBRASKA 68501

Editor	Consulting Editor
Gary Carey, M.A. *University of Colorado*	*James L. Roberts, Ph.D.* *Department of English* *University of Nebraska*

Cliffs Notes, Inc.   Lincoln, Nebraska

CONTENTS

BIOGRAPHICAL NOTE

Jerome David Salinger was born in New York City in 1919. His father was Sol Salinger, an importer of hams and cheeses. His mother was Marie Jillich, of Scotch-Irish descent, who changed her first name to Miriam when she married. There is presently no evidence to associate either of Salinger's parents with the theatre in any way. Undoubtedly, much of what he writes about is essentially autobiographical, but much of his life has little relation with his fiction. Salinger had no brothers and only one sister, Doris, eight years his senior. He attended public school on the Upper West Side in Manhattan, and his grades were average. Arithmetic was his worst subject. He was called "Sonny," and he is reported to have been a quiet, polite, solitary child. He spent his summers at Camp Wigwam in Harrison, Maine. When he was thirteen, his parents enrolled him in the McBurney School, but he flunked out within one year. When he was fifteen, he was sent to Valley Forge Military Academy in Pennsylvania. He graduated from that school in June 1936. While at Valley Forge he wrote his earliest stories. In 1937 he enrolled briefly at New York University, but his father took him to Vienna where he was to learn the ham business. He returned to the United States and enrolled in a short-story course offered by Whit Burnett, editor of *Story*. His first published story appeared in 1940. In 1942 Salinger was drafted into the Army. He spent his weekends in hotel rooms writing. In 1944 he was stationed in Tiverton, Devonshire, training in special counterintelligence work. On June 6, five hours after the "D Day" invasion began, Salinger landed with the 4th Infantry Division and remained with it through the Battle of the Bulge. His principal assignments were in intelligence. By 1946 Salinger had returned to New York, was discharged from the Army and divorced from a European woman doctor. In these years he lived with his parents on Park Avenue but spent most of his time in Greenwich Village where he was one of the early adherents of Zen. In the late 40's and early 50's, Salinger began a series of withdrawals, first to Tarrytown, then to Westport, and finally to Cornish, New Hampshire. He settled in the last city. At first he was friendly at least with the teenagers of the area, but he has withdrawn more and more. In 1953 he met Claire Douglas, and after a fairly stormy romance, married her in 1955. They have two children, Matthew and Peggy. Especially since his marriage, Salinger has withdrawn more and more from society. Part of his contemporary legend is based upon his isolation and his conscious and intentional separation of himself from his society.

INTRODUCTION

When *The Catcher in the Rye* first appeared, published by Little, Brown and Company, in 1951, it was received by critics and book reviewers as a literary sensation. Clifton Fadiman called it a "rare miracle of fiction," on the basis that, in his opinion, "...a human being [had] been created out of ink, paper and the imagination." The general opinion among other critics was similar to this one. There was hardly a dissenting voice. Since its publication, a large mass of critical opinion has grown up around this controversial novel. Some of the criticism has resulted from Salinger's use of profanity in the text. The book was banned in certain communities and condemned by some school boards. In the almost fifteen years since its publication, the book has acquired stout defenders and firm enemies.

Naturally, it is difficult to access the true value of a contemporary literary work. There is always some question about its popular reputation. How much of its reputation has been based, in this particular case, upon its contemporary notoriety? How much on its true literary value? Any writer who uses profanity for artistic purposes runs a serious risk of being misunderstood. This was certainly the case with D. H. Lawrence's *Lady Chatterley's Lover,* a book whose long career is marked by periodic obscenity and pornography trials. The late Aldous Huxley has pointed out that Lawrence simply forgot, in his attempts to portray reality, that readers have responses to such words, that obscenity is very old and that it has, in effect, a life of its own. This life of its own stands between the reader and the artist, and causes static in the reader's reception of the artist's intention. Something of the same sort occurs in *The Catcher in the Rye.*

Beyond that, *The Catcher in the Rye* is marked by other problems. It is certainly a "modern" novel. It is, in brief, the story of an adolescent boy on the brink of adulthood. Fiction concerned with this subject is by no means new. Salinger has been compared with Booth Tarkington (*Seventeen*) and with Mark Twain (*Huckleberry Finn*), and in so far as *The Catcher* is concerned with the problems of adolescence, the comparisons are valid. But it would also be possible to compare Salinger with James Joyce (*Portrait of the Artist as a Young Man*) and perhaps even with William Faulkner (*The Bear*), because *The Catcher* is perhaps more concerned with psychological pressures than it is with social pressures.

The concept of the hero in fiction has long been based upon Aristotle's definition:

> ...A man not pre-eminently virtuous and just, whose misfortune, however, is brought upon him not by vice or depravity, but by some error in judgement...The perfect plot, accordingly, must have a single...issue; the change in the hero's fortunes must be not from misery to happiness, but on the contrary from happiness to misery; and the cause of it must lie not in any depravity, but in some great error on his part....[1]

Such tragic heroes as Oedipus and Hamlet, Lear and Othello, Orestes and Macbeth are all examples of the Aristotelian definition in action. To be somewhat more specific, the tragic hero is a man, often an important man. At the beginning of the tragedy, he is happy. But as the tragedy develops, some failure in his personality begins to affect events, so that his progress is a movement from happiness to misery, and his ultimate misery is the result of his final awareness of the limit or the failure of his personality. Othello is a fairly good example of a tragic hero. At the opening of the story, he is just married. He is a respected hero, loved and admired by the people and the government. All circumstances point to the fact that he should be happy. And at first he is. But he has a flaw in his personality. He is a very jealous man. Iago sets about to destroy him, and it is really

---

[1] *The Poetics*, 13, in *Introduction to Aristotle*, ed. Richard McKeon [The Modern Library] (New York, 1947), p. 640.

a very easy matter. He plays upon Othello's jealousy. It is this passion, jealousy, that ultimately destroys the good and noble man Othello because it forces him to perform unreasonable acts, culminating in the murder of his wife. But, having committed that ultimate act, Othello recognizes that his overpowering jealousy rather than any external reality has led him to this act. Could he have believed that he had been right, he might have been able to endure any legal punishment for his act, but he realizes that he was wrong, and it is his realization of his own "tragic flaw" that is the most severe punishment. He was an essentially good man, but he was destroyed by his jealousy, by his error in judgment in trusting Iago. His progress is from happiness to abject misery, but the cause of his decline is not his own evil; it is only his tragic flaw in combination with his mistaken judgment. Modern literature does not seem to be concerned with heroes of this quality. Willie Loman in Arthur Miller's *Death of a Salesman* is the modern "hero." By Aristotle's definition, he is not a hero at all because he is not tragic, merely pathetic. Modern literature seems to be far more concerned with the "low man" than with the hero. Modern heroes come from the ranks of ordinary life; they are not great men, kings, princes, generals. They are salesmen, schoolteachers (Bernard Malmud's *A New Life*), bums (Kerouac's *On the Road*) and other similar types in the novels of William Styron, James Jones, John O'Hara, Carson McCullers, and others as well as in the plays of Tennessee Williams, Eugene O'Neill, William Inge, and others. These modern heroes are not men with the flaw; rather, they are victims. Their failures are not the results of personal depravity. They are not bad men. But neither are their failures the results of some fault in judgment. Quite the contrary, these modern heroes are victims of society, an inevitable force which crushes and destroys them, and the modern novelists hold up these specimens pinned to the psychiatrist's couch like insects in museum display cases. Sometimes their very reality depends upon psychological case history more than it does on innate humanity.

Holden Caulfield belongs to this new category of hero. He is a victim of his society. He is "depressed" over the great abundance of "phonies" in the world; even his admired brother D. B. has sold out to Hollywood. *The Catcher in the Rye* is, superficially, Holden's personal narrative of his four day attempt to find a fixed reality, free of the adult "phoniness" which limits the *demi-monde* of the adolescent. At the same time, it is an odyssey — at least as much so as *Huckleberry Finn* or *Ulysses* — seeking, metaphorically, a home for the contemporary psyche free of the seductions of the modern Circe, advertising, the dangers of the modern Scylla and Charybdis, television and the movie, and so on. Ulysses, returning from the Trojan wars, wants only to get back to his home. He is delayed because he simply gets lost — spiritually as well as geographically. Huck Finn goes down the river with Jim to seek freedom — a new home where the injustices of the old life will not exist. Holden too is seeking a new home — a place where it will be possible for him to become involved with people and with life without the inevitable pain and disillusionment that seems to come with involvement. Holden seeks his new home in the adult world "beyond" the limits of his adolescent experience. Like Huck and Ulysses, he meets tests and dangers on his voyage, but while the tests and dangers for Huck and Ulysses were physical, the dangers that Holden encounters are metaphorical dangers created out of the contemporary mass culture and the standard manifestations of that culture — the loss of individuality, of accepted values, of intellectual autonomy.

All of this is an attempt to place *The Catcher* in a frame of reference which will make further discussion of it meaningful. No book, after all, exists in a vacuum, but every book is a part of a long literary tradition which in itself shapes and molds the writer and his art. *The Catcher* is a mid-twentieth century book, but it is also a product of the tradition of English literature.

GENERAL PLOT SUMMARY

These notes are designed as a supplement to *The Catcher in the Rye,* and not as a substitute for the book. A plot summary of this novel is particularly difficult to make meaningful, because the book is episodic in character. In its over-all structure, it is a first-person narration, in the form of a "confession"; a patient's oral statement to his psychoanalyst. The whole novel is a "flashback" filled with digressions and character-revealing asides. What is vital is not the action itself, but the psychological states of the narrator, an emotionally disturbed sixteen-year old boy. A plot summary cannot possibly recreate the detail, the language, or the effect of the original; it can only restate the superficialities of the action.

The book consists of twenty-six units which might loosely be called chapters. These chapters range in length from a few lines to as much as fifteen pages. The entire book covers, in retrospect, a time-span of four days, but the time of given chapters varies, expanding and contracting as remembered events become significant not in their duration but in their effect. The book is framed between the first and last chapters which take place in some sort of mental hospital in California. A great many persons are mentioned (about fifty in all). Some have more or less active parts while others are mentioned only in passing.

The large number of characters suggests that a world is involved. Holden Caulfield does not inhabit a literary vacuum. He is a character with a great many acquaintances, like most contemporary urban citizens. The site of the principal action is New York City, and the city itself takes on the part of a character; that is, it is not merely a backdrop against which the action occurs. Central Park, The American Museum of Natural History, and the Metropolitan Museum of Art are real places in a real city. They form the borders of a world—Holden's world, but they also act upon him. The unnamed characters who are scattered through the book are aspects of the City. Salinger has created a world in the same sense that Dickens created a world, and the reference to David Copperfield in the fourth line of the novel is no accident. Dicken's incidental characters are grotesques of the urban world of the Industrial Revolution; Salinger's are grotesques of the urban world of the Atomic Age.

CAST OF CHARACTERS

CAULFIELD FAMILY

Allie
Holden's brother, died of leukemia July 18, 1946, 2 years younger than Holden.

D. B.
Holden's elder brother, a poet who is now "out in Hollywood ...being a prostitute."

Holden
The narrator

Mother, Father, Grandmother, and Aunt

Phoebe
Holden's sister, 10 years old.

TEACHERS

Miss Aigletinger
Holden's grade school teacher.

Mr. Antolini and his Wife
English teacher at Elkton Hills.

Mr. Spencer and his Wife
History teacher at Pencey Prep.

Mr. Vinson
Oral Expression teacher at Pencey Prep.

SCHOOL FRIENDS

Robert Ackley
Student at Pencey Prep.

Ward Stradlater
Holden's roommate at Pencey.

Mal Brossard
Student at Pencey.

Jane Gallagher
Old girl friend of Holden's.

Sally Hayes
A girl with whom Holden has a date.

James Castle
Student at Elkton Hills who committed suicide.

Ely
Ackley's roommate.

Lillian Simmons
A girl previously dated by D. B.

George something
Andover student, friend of Sally Hayes.

Carl Luce
Student at Whooton.

Al Pike, Bob Robinson, Roberta Walsh, Richard Kinsella
Various other students.

A few other persons are mentioned, more or less in passing, and although some of them are named, they are so minor as not to need separate mention.

CHAPTER I

Summary

Holden Caulfield is introduced as the speaker. The scene is a "rest home" in California, and Holden is telling the story of the subsequent events in a long flashback. In the flashback, Holden was a student at Pencey Prep, a boy's school in Pennsylvania. The flashback begins on a Saturday afternoon four days before the beginning of the Christmas vacation. Holden, having been expelled from the school, is not at the game. He is on his way to pay a final visit to Mr. Spencer, his history teacher.

Commentary

The first chapter immediately introduces Holden as the speaker. The opening sentence of the novel captures and develops the tricks of speech that characterize Holden as a "modern teenager": These include 1) the consistent use of such expressions as *lousy, crap, and all, if you want to know the truth;* 2) the use of direct address; 3) the negative and rebellious tone (later Mr. Antolini is to say: "...I can very clearly see you dying nobly, one way or another, for some highly unworthy cause."); 4) the use of nouns for adjectives (David Copperfield kind of crap); 5) and the use of slang nouns generally quite imprecise in meaning (*crap, stuff*). In general, the chapter places Holden in the psychiatric hospital in California, introduces Pencey Prep as one of a long series of private schools which have failed Holden, mentions his brother D. B., and begins to develop one of the central themes of the book: what might be called Holden's war against phonies. He finds his own prep school, "Pencey Prep," to be one of the worst phonies. "Strictly for the birds. They don't do any damn more molding at Pencey than they do at any other school." In contrast to the phonies, Holden is honest in spite of himself. Exaggeration ("about a thousand magazines") is a common device for him, and so is lying, but he cannot help being honest, at least with himself ("Maybe two guys").

The first chapter initiates the device of the flashback which occupies the whole book, and as in the sentence already quoted, introduces the digressions typical of Holden's thinking. Holden cannot organize his thoughts. He has trouble selecting what is important out of a body of information (the principal reason for Freshman Composition courses in colleges and universities). Since he seems incapable of selection, his talk approaches stream-of-consciousness, although of course it is a stream carefully controlled by Salinger to present his point. Holden's speech, furthermore, has the ring of authenticity. There is no question that Salinger knows the speech he is mimicking. To say the least, Salinger has an excellent ear for dialect. The writing of believable dialect is extremely difficult, and the most skillful of novelists have failed in the attempt.

The events here are on many time levels, but the story being told begins here in the middle of a Saturday afternoon just a few days prior to the start of the Christmas holidays. The novel covers four days on this time level.

CHAPTER II

Summary

Holden visits Mr. Spencer who is sick in bed. Mr. Spencer lectures Holden on his poor scholarship and even reads Holden his own last examination paper. Holden feels sorry for Mr. Spencer, but he is glad to leave after their interview.

Commentary

In this chapter, Holden has his interview with Mr. Spencer, the history teacher at Pencey. "Old Spencer" is in bed suffering from the grippe. Holden provides the reader with a brief "character" of Spencer before the interview takes place. The Spencers were the type who "got a bang out of things," but "in a half-assed way." Mr. Spencer was so old that when he dropped his chalk, a student had to pick it up for him. "That's awful, in my opinion. But if you thought about him just enough and not *too* much, you could figure it out that he wasn't doing too bad for himself...."

Obviously, in his own way, Holden has admired Spencer, yet he says, "The minute I went in [to his room], I was sort of sorry I'd come." Through the course of the interview, Spencer reveals himself as an ordinary man with ordinary failings. He subjects Holden to the pain of listening to his own examination question. As he reads, Holden says, "I was beginning to sort of hate him." The climax of the scene develops as Spencer imposes the ultimate indignity on Holden by forcing him to listen even to the note he appended to his examination answer. Holden can't forgive Mr. Spencer for reading "that crap out loud. I wouldn't've read it out loud to *him* if *he'd* written it — I really wouldn't."

The first of Holden's illusions has been stripped away from him, and the end of the section is pathetic and dreary as Holden realizes that the old man was simply trying to help. There is, however, too much difference between them. "I felt sorry as hell for him...but I just couldn't hang around there any longer, the way we were on opposite sides of the pole."

Spencer's facade has been stripped away by his illness, and Holden's odyssey has begun.

CHAPTER III

Summary

Holden returns to his room in Ossenburger Memorial Hall. He provides a brief background of Mr. Ossenburger, lists some of the books that he has enjoyed reading, and explains that he is presently reading *Out of Africa*. Robert Ackley, the boy in the neighboring room, comes in to visit Holden. They talk at some length about school matters. The conversation is interrupted by the arrival of Ward Stradlater, Holden's roommate.

Commentary

The third chapter opens with a brief discussion of the fact that Holden is quite a liar. It suggests a certain tendency toward neurotic *self*-deception which will be developed later. The section introduces a logic problem; if Holden *is* a liar, as he claims, then it is possible that much of what he is telling is untrue; but if Holden is not really a liar, then the statement that he is a liar cannot be quite true. This logical problem is a key to Holden's psychological situation in the sense that his thinking often leads him to ambiguity and confusion. The entire chapter takes place in Holden's room in Ossenburger Hall. After the confession about being a liar, a relatively long section is devoted to a digression on Ossenburger, who is a kind of Babbitt figure. Still another digression details Holden's reading habits. His favorite author is his brother D. B., but he likes Ring Lardner, Thomas Hardy, and Isak Dinesen, whom he is currently reading. He has read Somerset Maugham's *Of Human Bondage,* but thinks that Somerset Maugham" just isn't the kind of guy" that he would want to call up.

The remainder of the chapter is devoted to a conversation between Holden and Ackley. Again Ackley is described as a senior who has spent all four years at Pencey Prep. He was very tall with stooped shoulders, bad teeth, and lots of pimples. "Not just on his forehead or his chin, like most guys, but all over his whole face." He is summed up as being a "sort of a nasty guy."

But, grotesque as he is, Ackley is a boarding-school type. The characterization is in the best tradition of Dickensian grotesques. Although Holden isn't "too crazy" about him, they do seem to be friends after a fashion. Holden at least tolerates Ackley. Perhaps their mutual isolation draws the two boys together, although, of course, the isolation stems from quite different causes. The conversation is pointless, heavy with schoolboy sarcasm and the terrible cruelty of the helpless vented against the equally helpless. (This sort of cruelty is not to be confused with the savagery depicted in Golding's *Lord of the Flies*.)

The chapter ends with the breezy arrival of Ward Stradlater, Holden's roommate, who is described as having an outgoing personality and a good body build which even Holden has to admire.

CHAPTER IV

Summary
Holden and Stradlater hold a long conversation, partly in their room, and partly in the latrine, during which Holden learns that Stradlater 1) is back to get ready for a date; 2) has a date with a girl that Holden knows and likes, Jane Gallagher; 3) wants Holden to write a descriptive theme for him. Stradlater leaves and Ackley returns.

Commentary
This chapter concerns a dialogue between Stradlater and Holden. It takes place partly in the latrine and partly in the dormitory room. Stradlater has a date, and he has come back to clean up, shave, borrow Holden's hound's-tooth jacket, and generally prepare himself for his date. In the course of the conversation, Holden learns that Stradlater's date is with Jane Gallagher, a girl whom he knows and likes. Holden is concerned for the girl, since he believes Stradlater to be "a sexy bastard." In the course of the conversation, too, Stradlater has asked Holden to write his homework theme for him, and Holden has partially agreed to do it. The conversation is desultory, illustrating the general boredom which is a part of Holden's life. The boredom is inherent in the boarding school situation, but many boys find ways to escape it: Athletics, scholarship, sex, cam-

pus politics. But Holden finds all of these to be inherently "phony" as practiced, and he is bored with them as well. After Holden learns that Jane Gallagher is Stradlater's date, he becomes excited and even suggests that he might go down to the "Annex" and say hello to her. But he finds that he isn't "in the mood right now." He gives Stradlater a great deal of background information about her, but Stradlater is only interested in the "sexy" items. Much of what Holden has to say about her reveals the basic humanity both of Holden and of the girl, but these things pass by Stradlater. Holden asks Stradlater to give Jane his regards, and Stradlater promises to do so, but Holden is sure he won't. As Stradlater leaves, Holden's tension begins to build up as he continues to think about Stradlater's dating Jane. His thoughts are interrupted by the second arrival of Ackley who enlightens Holden by "talking about all the guys at Pencey that he hated their guts, and squeezing this big pimple on his chin."

CHAPTER V

Summary

Holden has dinner in the dormitory—the same steak dinner served every Saturday. Then he and Mal Brossard and Ackley go into town. They plan to see a movie but discover that Ackley and Brossard have already seen it. Then they have hamburgers and play the pin ball machines for a while. They return to campus just before nine, and Ackley joins Holden in his room while Brossard goes off in search of a bridge game. Finally, Ackley goes away, and Holden writes the composition for Stradlater. The composition describes Holden's brother's baseball glove. By ten-thirty he is finished.

Commentary

The fifth chapter concerns the bulk of the remainder of Saturday evening. The Saturday evening meal is described in some detail. It is always tough, dry steak, and Holden speculates about the motivation behind this sameness. After dinner, Mal Brossard, a boy on the wrestling team, and Holden catch a bus into Agerstown: They plan to "...have a hamburger and maybe see a lousy movie. Neither of us felt like sitting around on our ass all night." Holden, out of sympathy for Ackley ("...because Ackley never did anything on Saturday night, except stay in his room and squeeze his pimples or something"), invites him to go along. Brossard and Ackley have already seen the picture, so after eating a hamburger and playing the pinball machine, they return to the dormitory.

The monotony of this routine, the boredom of this life, the triviality of conversation and action all suggest the things that are crushing Holden. He is caught in the middle-class morality and the middle-class assumptions of values and aims with which he is totally out of sympathy, which he considers essentially and inherently "phony."

Holden finally succeeds in getting rid of Ackley, who has been regaling him with tales of his sexual life (imaginary). After Ackley has gone, Holden sits down to compose the descriptive theme he has promised to write for Stradlater, but he couldn't think of anything that would fit the subject described to him. Therefore, he decides to write a description of his brother Allie's left-handed baseball mitt. "The thing that was descriptive about it, though, was that he had poems written all over the fingers and the pocket and everywhere. In green ink."

The section provides a long digression on Allie, detailing his life and death. The significant point comes at the conclusion of the digression when Holden narrates his own reaction to Allie's death. After telling how he broke windows and slept in the garage on the night of Allie's death, he admits it was a stupid thing to do, but adds that "you didn't know Allie." The *you* addressed in the last sentence of this section is, of course, the person (psychologist, analyst) to whom Holden is telling the whole story; the hearer in the rest home in California; but the *you* is, also, the reader. This device permits Salinger to address the reader directly, thus making the book much more personal and less clinical, while at the same time it permits the illusion of the story line.

The composition is finished by about ten-thirty. Holden, not tired, spends some time looking out the window at the snow scene.

CHAPTER VI

Summary
Stradlater returns from his date. He does not like the composition. Holden, already upset because Stradlater dated Jane Gallagher,

destroys the composition. An argument flares up between the two boys, and finally Holden strikes Stradlater. There is a fight, and Holden is beaten. Ultimately, Stradlater leaves the room, and Holden goes next door to see Ackley.

Commentary

Holden's meditation is interrupted by the return of Stradlater from his date. The tension that has been building in Holden as a result of his "nervousness" in Chapter IV and his boredom in Chapters IV and V now explodes into an unaccustomed action. "Some things are hard to remember," says Holden. The sequence of action is hazy in his mind. He does not recall where he was when Stradlater came in. Stradlater comes in "griping about how cold it was out." He starts to undress. As he does so he asks Holden whether he has written the theme for him. When Holden tells Stradlater that the finished theme is on his bed, Stradlater reads it and becomes infuriated. He attacks Holden with various accusations. In the face of this burst of almost irrational anger, Holden acts. "I went over and pulled it right out of his goddam hand. Then I tore it up." This action effectively closes the conversation, and in stony silence, the two boys go about their respective activities. Holden lies in bed smoking, in part at least to annoy Stradlater. Stradlater continues to undress. The tension increases until Holden finally says: "You're back pretty goddam late if she only signed out for nine-thirty. Did you make her be late signing in?" Some conversation on this general subject follows, during which Stradlater cuts his toe nails and subsequently comes "...over to my bed and started leaning over me and taking these playful as hell socks at my shoulder." Holden's curiosity and concern overcome his control. He demands to know what happened in the back seat of the car. Stadlater tells him that it's a "professional secret." That answer leads directly to the first climax of the book. It is important to remember that the time is approximately eleven-thirty Saturday night. The conversation leading up to this climax reveals the relative inexperience of the two boys. Stradlater is unconscious of Holden's concern. He does not understand Holden. Holden, on the other hand, is unable to read the frustration in Stradlater's anger over the theme, and his general irritation in reference to the weather, the state of the dorm, and so on. Two totally different worlds are represented, and the bridging of the gap between them is literally impossible.

In any case, the climax arrives when Holden tries to strike Stradlater. In the ensuing fight, Stradlater, the bigger, more athletic boy, shows remarkable restraint. At least he is not a bully. He does not try to hurt Holden, but only to restrain him. Of course, the humiliation of being restrained spurs Holden on to insult and profanity to the point at which Stradlater, in order to preserve his own self-image, really must hit Holden. That ends the fight, for Holden is hurt and bleeding, and he has vented his spleen in words, and Stradlater is frightened over the damage he has done. The important point is that Stradlater never understands why Holden attacked him. But Holden, lying on the floor, bleeding and cursing, is "…so mad, [he] was practically bawling." Stradlater finally leaves the room. Holden, having examined himself in the mirror ("it partly scared me and it partly fascinated me."), goes to Ackley's room.

CHAPTER VII

Summary

Ackley has heard the fight, but he is not terribly interested nor terribly sympathetic. He wants to go to sleep, and Holden wants to talk. Finally, Holden leaves the room planning to look for Brossard, but at that moment he decides to leave the school at once. He returns to his room, finishes packing, and leaves.

Commentary

Ackley has heard the fight, and he is curious, but he is by no means sympathetic. He does not understand what the fight is about. Ackley is a Catholic, and his concern is to be allowed to go to sleep so that he can get up in time to go to mass. Since he does not understand what underlies the situation, he is anxious to get rid of Holden. Once he has assured Holden that he does not wish to play cards, to talk, nor to have Holden sleep in his room, he goes back to sleep. Holden wakes him again with a question about joining a monastic order, but Ackley, not understanding, is indignant.

Holden leaves the room, planning to go and see what Brossard is doing, but on his way he changes his mind and decides to leave the school immediately. He returns to his room, packs his belongings (already partially packed since Christmas vacation begins on the following Wednesday, and Holden has been invited not to return after the holidays), counts his money, and leaves. As he is ready to leave, he is tempted into one last act of foolish bravado. This is, in fact, the end of a chapter in Holden's life, and he is aware of it. "I was sort of crying. I don't know why." He then turns and yells *"Sleep tight, ya morons,"* so loudly that he wakes everyone up. That would have been a good place to close the chapter, but Holden has one more fact to report; one more instance of the inhumanity of man to man: "Some stupid guy had thrown peanut shells all over the stairs, and I damn near broke my crazy neck."

CHAPTER VIII

Summary
Holden walks to the train station. Once there he cleans off the blood from the fight with snow, and in a few minutes catches a train for New York. The train is relatively deserted. He meets a woman who turns out to be the mother of one of his classmates. They have some general conversation.

Commentary
Holden walks to the station, because it is too late to call a taxi. The walk gives him a chance to cool down. At the station he finds that he will only need to wait about ten minutes for a train to New York. He spends the waiting time cleaning the blood from his face with snow. A small digression provides the information that he usually likes riding trains at night, but not this time.

The first adventure of his new life involves a woman. She is not young, and she turns out to be the mother of one of his classmates, but she is attractive. The contact is innocent enough; nothing more than a brief conversation, but it gives Holden a chance to be suave and sophisticated, at least in his own eyes. Unfortunately, he begins to lie about himself and, typically, gets overinvolved in his lies. His lies tend to romanticize him. In this sense, in his verbalized daydreams, he is a kind of Walter Mitty. He lies to the mother about her son too, but these lies are perpetrated out of kindness. The mother then invites him to visit them during the summer, but Holden "wouldn't visit that sonova-bitch Morrow for all the dough in the world."

CHAPTER IX

Summary

Arriving in New York's Penn Station, Holden considers calling someone, but decides it is too late. He takes a taxi to the Edmont Hotel, an older hotel. Once in his room he discovers that he can see activities in rooms across from his. He watches for a time and then decides to call Jane Gallagher. He changes his mind and calls Faith Cavendish, but the call is unproductive.

Commentary

Arriving at Penn Station in New York, Holden goes into a phone booth to call someone — anyone, but considering the hour and the probabilities, he finally calls no one. He gets a taxi, giving his home address, but then corrects himself and asks to be taken to the Edmont Hotel. On the way he asks the cab driver if he knows what happens to the ducks in the lake in Central Park during the winter. The cab driver does not understand. At the hotel, Holden is given a "very crumby room, with nothing to look out of the window at except the other side of the hotel." The place is full of "perverts and morons," he discovers. The bellhop is elderly, and to Holden is "even more depressing than the room itself." After the elderly bell-hop leaves, Holden looks out the window for a while, simply because he has nothing else to do. It is his intention to remain in hiding until Wednesday when he can legitimately go home. In the rooms across the court, a female impersonator is dressing, and a couple of people are squirting water at each other. Holden finds that "...that kind of junk is fascinating to watch, even if you don't want it to be.... "And this leads him to a reasonably accurate self-analysis: he thinks that he is the "biggest sex maniac you ever saw," but later admits that he really doesn't understand sex or know much about it.

Holden, however, finds himself feeling rather "horny," and decides and undecides to call Jane Gallagher. Instead, he calls a girl named Faith Cavendish. Her name and address were given to Holden by a fellow who went to Princeton. She "wasn't exactly a whore or anything, but [she] didn't mind doing it once in a while...." The conversation is long, and Holden is again suave and sophisticated at least in his own eyes, but it comes to nothing. "Boy," says Holden, "I *really* fouled that up." Another incursion into the adult world, or what Holden considers to be the adult world, has been thwarted, in part because Holden doesn't really know the rules—he is only guessing at them—and in part because loneliness is not a substitute for experience. Holden is a mid-twentieth century innocent—a virgin by his own confession—not only in matters of sex, but in orientation to the code of the practical world of material achievement and success.

CHAPTER X

Summary

It is still Saturday night. Holden is not sleepy, so he changes and goes down to the "club" in the Hotel. There he meets three secretaries from Seattle, Washington. He spends some time dancing with them, and leaves the club shortly after they do.

Commentary

It is still Saturday night, gradually becoming Sunday morning. Unable to sleep, Holden changes his shirt and goes to the Lavender Room, a club in the hotel. There is a long digression on his sister Phoebe. Holden wants to call her on the phone, but he is afraid his parents will answer. In any case, Holden's sincere and deep attachment to and respect for his sister is obvious in this digression.

Following the digression, he goes to the club. He is put at a bad table, and the waiter refuses to serve him alcohol. Three women at the next table catch his attention. He returns their stares until they begin giggling at him; in fact, "they started giggling like morons...." However, in spite of the discouragement and embarrassment, because he "really felt like dancing," Holden forges ahead and does manage to get them to dance with him. The conversation, or lack of it, is even more enervating than the empty and pointless latrine-bull-sessions of earlier chapters. One of the three dances well — "Bernice something — Crabs or Krebs" — but she is vacuous. Holden is savagely satiric in his conversation, but most of his satire escapes her. In spite of his sarcasm, however, Holden was "about half in love with her" at the end of the dance, and when they sat down, he was feeling rather strange and awkward. "Girls, Jesus Christ. They can drive you crazy. They really can." The other two, Marty and Laverne, are not even good dancers. All three are secretaries from Seattle, Washington, and they are constantly on the look-out for movie stars. Intelligent conversation is impossible. They are provincial, but they are wise enough to leave the check for Holden. They retire because they plan to go to Radio City Music Hall early the next morning. This makes Holden feel depressed because he can't understand why someone would come all the way from Washington just to get up early to see some stupid building. Holden leaves the club shortly after the girls from Seattle leave because nightclubs are depressing unless a person can buy some drinks or unless he is with some really beautiful girl.

CHAPTER XI

Summary
Back in the hotel lobby, he sits down and thinks about Jane Gallagher, but he finds the process very depressing. He is genuinely concerned about the girl's experience with Stradlater.

Commentary
As he leaves the club and comes back into the lobby, occupied by "...a few pimpy-looking guys, and a few whory-looking blondes, ..." Holden starts thinking about Jane Gallagher again. He sits down in a "vomity-looking chair in the lobby" and thinks about her. The bulk of the chapter is a long digression on a previous summer when Holden knew Jane. The digression shows Jane as a sensitive girl who lives with her mother and stepfather. Her stepfather, a Mr. Cudahy, appears to be a pretty unpleasant fellow, and Holden has been moved enormously by Jane's difficult situation. But Holden confuses his enormous sympathy for Jane with other emotions.

He does not himself understand the nature of his feelings: every-time he thinks about Jane and Stradlater, it almost drives him crazy. In fact, he doesn't want to think about it or talk about it any more.

In this state of mind, Holden cannot go to bed. He calls a cab and goes to Ernie's, a Greenwich Village club where D. B. used to take him, "before he went out to Hollywood and prostituted him-self." The chapter ends with a small digression about Ernie, a piano player who is "so good he's almost corny." This is a value judgment that Holden cannot explain, but he is aware of the rightness of it.

CHAPTER XII

Summary
Holden takes a taxi to Ernie's, a Greenwich Village nightclub. The club is crowded, and Holden is given a bad table. While there he encounters a girl named Lillian Simmons who had dated Hol-den's older brother D. B., presently a writer in Hollywood. She is with a naval officer. After the encounter, Holden leaves.

Commentary
In the taxi on the way to Ernie's, Holden gets into conversa-tion with Horowitz, the cab driver, over the question of the ducks in Central Park. This driver responds much more dramatically than the anonymous cab driver in Chapter IX, and he provides a heated series of comments. Holden's recurrent concern for the ducks is in-dicative of his personality—one characterized by concern for what appears trivial and inconsequential to many. Horowitz changes the conversation from the ducks to the fish, because he can cope with them, and Horowitz is a believer in the rightness of things. His part-ing comment: "Listen,...if you was a fish, Mother Nature'd take care of *you*, wouldn't she? Right? You don't think them fish just *die* when it gets to be winter, do ya?...You're goddam right they don't...." clarifies his thinking completely.

Ernie's is quite crowded, largely with prep school and college students already free for Christmas. Ernie himself is playing when Holden arrives, and Holden provides another digression on the quality of Ernie's talent. It seems that Ernie is playing some fancy additions to the tune and including many extra notes. The audience is quite impressed and cheers for a long time. Holden finds this to be very phony and he nearly gets sick. He concludes that even Ernie doesn't know when he is playing well anymore, and this thought depresses Holden.

Holden gets a table in a corner, a bad table, and he orders a drink. Ernie's waiters are not particular about matters of age. While having his drink, Holden listens in to a conversation at the adjoining table. The couple at that table are relatively unattractive, and the conversation produces another typical Holden comment: "Real ugly girls have it tough. I feel so sorry for them sometimes. Sometimes I can't even look at them, especially if they're with some dopey guy that's telling them all about a goddam football game." The conversation on the other side of him is worse because the guy is "giving" his girl "a feel" and at the same time is telling her about some person who attempted to commit suicide by taking too many aspirins.

Suddenly a girl who had known his older brother comes over to Holden's table. She has a naval officer in tow. The conversation is typical of the situation—small talk. The girl invites Holden to join them for a drink, but he tells her he was just leaving. A brief aside comments on the absurdity of formal greeting of strangers. Having said that he was leaving, Holden feels he must be honest and leave. "It made me mad, though.... People are always ruining things for you."

CHAPTER XIII

Summary

Holden walks back to his hotel. During the walk, since it is very cold, Holden thinks about his gloves which he believes to have been stolen at school. Along the way, Holden considers going into a bar, but he is discouraged by the emergence of two unsavory men. Back at the hotel, Holden is solicited by the elevator operator who promises to get him a prostitute. He accepts, and goes to his room to prepare himself. The girl arrives, but Holden is too frightened and embarrassed to participate. Finally he sends the girl away.

Commentary

On the walk back to the hotel, Holden starts thinking about his gloves. He believes that they were stolen. He pictures to himself a confrontation with the thief, but he is realist enough to be well aware that although he might feel like striking the perpetrator of the theft, the confrontation would end up in extended sarcasm and no action. He pictures himself as a coward. These speculations are significant in terms of what happens in the following section. As he gets nearer to the hotel, he contemplates going in to what he describes as a "dumpy-looking bar." He is discouraged by the appearance of two drunks, one a "very Cuban-looking guy," from the bar. Instead he simply goes back to the hotel.

One of the key incidents in the book is introduced by the line: "Then all of a sudden, I got in this big mess." The elevator operator asks Holden if he wants a girl. Holden is startled by the directness of the approach: "...its quite embarrassing when somebody comes right up and asks you a question like that." However, Holden accepts the proposition, first assuring himself that the girl will be reasonably attractive. He returns to his room to wait for her and to prepare himself—an indication of his naiveté. While describing his wait he makes a series of significant confessions. First, he admits that he is pretty nervous about sex. Then, he confesses that he is actually a virgin. Holden tells us that he has had opportunities, but has just never gotten around to actually losing his virginity. Therefore, he thinks that maybe now is a good time to get some practice just in case he ever gets married.

Interspersed with these confessions are speculations of another sort. Holden describes a previous occasion on which he nearly lost his virginity. He complains that when one comes close to achieving intercourse with a girl who is not a prostitute, the girl always protests and asks the boy to stop. Holden confesses that he does stop, because he is unsure whether or not the girl really means it. At this point, his attitude is reminiscent of the attitude expressed by T. S. Eliot in the "Lovesong of J. Alfred Prufrock." Holden's attitude is very similar to Prufrock's in the fear of hurting someone. Holden's hyper-humanitarian attitudes spoil most of his pose. Again, he confesses that when he is out with a girl and she tells him to stop, he always does. After he gets home, he always wishes that he hadn't stopped, but he always does stop.

Still interspersed with the confessions is a memory of a book Holden once read. The book is about a Monsieur Blanchard, a rake. Holden is impressed with his knowledge and adds another important confession. It is important to remember, at this point, that the frame of the book is the psychiatrist's couch. Here his confession is more concrete. He explains that he can't find what he is looking for when he is with a girl. Once he had a girl who was about ready for intercourse, and he couldn't even find out how to unfasten her brassiere. Finally, the girl arrives, and Holden greets her with his customary suavity, although he tripped over his suitcase getting to the door. The girl is not impressed. She is all business. The conversation is neither suave nor brilliant. Holden is impressed with her youth, her lack of either sophistication on the one hand or hardness on the other. She slips off her clothes and says "Let's go, hey." Holden is overcome with embarrassment. He suggests that they talk a while. The girl says "What the heck ya wanna talk about?" She considers Holden quite mad. Finally, after several abortive attempts at conversation, Holden suggests they forget the whole thing. "The trouble was, I just didn't want to do it. I felt more depressed than sexy, if you want to know the truth. *She* was depressing." Holden starts to lie to get rid of the girl, but she begins to show signs of interest. She sits on his lap. Finally Holden convinces her that he is not interested. He pays her the five dollars that he and the elevator operator had agreed upon, but she says its ten dollars. Holden refuses to pay more than five and finally gets her to leave. Several times during the closing moments of the scene, Holden comments on his own nervousness.

CHAPTER XIV

Summary

Holden smokes a few cigarettes and goes to bed. Maurice, the elevator operator, and Sonny, the prostitute, return. They want the other five dollars. Holden refuses to pay it, and Maurice threatens him. Sonny and Maurice get their money, and Maurice abuses Holden. Subsequently, they leave, and Holden finally goes to bed after spending some time daydreaming.

Commentary

After the prostitute leaves, Holden starts thinking about his brother Allie. It will be remembered that Allie has been mentioned earlier in connection with his baseball glove, in Chapter V. Holden is trying to make up for an injustice committed years ago. He does it when he gets very depressed. Holden goes to bed but he cannot sleep. He feels that he wants to pray, but he can't. A fairly long digression is introduced on religion in which Holden contrasts his own faith with institutionalized faiths. He feels that "...Jesus never sent old Judas to hell....I think any one of the *Disciples* would've sent him to hell and all—and fast, too—but I'll bet anything Jesus didn't do it." He also feels that ministers have "Holy Joe voices." "They sound so phony when they talk."

Still unable to sleep, Holden smokes another cigarette. While he is smoking, Sonny and Maurice return to claim the other five dollars. Maurice intimidates Holden while Sonny takes exactly the amount due her. The conversation is depressing, and Holden is exposed to a new reality with which he has been unfamiliar. Maurice is a bully and something of a sadist. After Sonny has gotten her money, Maurice gratuitously hurts Holden, and when Holden replies with his tongue, which is characteristic of him, Maurice hits him. The scene is a repetition of the earlier scene with Stradlater. Again Holden is incapable of dealing with physical brutality. Again, Holden is reduced to tears and profanity. Again, Holden's attitude is akin to the attitude of the martyrs, acting in such a way that physical reaction is inevitable and then not attempting to avoid the physical reaction—in fact, welcoming it.

After Maurice and Sonny leave, Holden projects himself into a movie hero. He imagines that he has been shot, that he is a "tough-guy," that he is crawling to the bathroom for a drink which will give him the impetus to real action. Even while he indulges in these fantasies, he is aware that they are fantasies. "The goddam movies. They can ruin you. I'm not kidding."

Finally, after taking a bath, Holden goes back to bed and again tries to sleep. But he has difficulty falling asleep. Sunday morning is dawning outside. A period of about fifteen hours has elapsed since the beginning of the story. An enormous amount of experience has been packed into those hours. At the beginning of this chapter, Holden had wanted to pray. Now, his attitude has changed again; he feels like committing suicide. But he refrains because he is afraid that no one would cover up his body after he is dead and he doesn't "want a bunch of stupid rubbernecks looking at me when I was all gory."

The second climax has been reached.

CHAPTER XV

Summary

Holden wakes up relatively early Sunday morning. He calls Sally Hayes for a date that day. Then, since he is running short of money, he checks out of the hotel. He takes a taxi to Grand Central Station where he checks his bags in a locker and then eats breakfast in a small cafeteria in the station. While eating breakfast he meets two nuns, teachers from Chicago being transferred to a New York convent. Holden gives them a contribution and they have a fairly lengthy conversation about general topics.

Commentary

When Holden awakens in the hotel room, he finds that he is rather hungry. He ate last in Agerstown with Ackley and Brossard just before nine o'clock the previous evening. He considers calling room-service for breakfast, but remembering Maurice and the events of the night before decides against it. He also considers phoning Jane Gallagher again, but he isn't "in the mood." An enormous number of phone calls do not get made in this book. Holden often considers calling someone but finds that he isn't in the mood. It is possible that the uncompleted phone calls serve as a symbol of the broken communication between Holden and the vast majority of people. He does, however, call Sally Hayes, and he makes a date with her for two o'clock that afternoon. It is curious that he does not really like Sally. "She gave me a pain in the ass, but she was very good looking."

Holden now has four or five hours to kill before his date. He dressed, checked out of the hotel (without encountering Maurice), and took a taxi to Grand Central Station simply because he had no other place to go. Grand Central is the main railroad station in New York City. It is the home of the transient. Before the time of jet travel, it was the transportation center of New York. Its importance as a center cannot be overstressed. It is the meeting place of commuters, the hub from which both business and social affairs begin. But it is a restless place. Nothing is permanent there. No one *stays* there; rather, everyone passes through there. It is perhaps significant of Holden's state of mind that he selects it as the place to go. In any case, he does go there. He checks his bags in a locker and then goes to have breakfast. He is aware that his money is becoming rapidly depleted. As he is having his breakfast in a transient cafeteria, Holden encounters two nuns. The scene with the nuns is quite interesting. Holden is filled with pity for them in a strange way. He gives them ten dollars out of his rapidly diminishing stock of money. He attempts to buy their breakfasts, but they do not permit him to do so. He indulges in a long digression on the subject of hand baggage. The nuns had "...these very inexpensive-looking suitcases — the ones that aren't genuine leather or anything. It isn't important, I know, but I hate it when somebody has cheap suitcases." Holden narrates an incident from his stay at Elkton Hills School. His roommate, Dick Slagle, had cheap suitcases which he hid under the bed. He insisted that Holden display his suitcases on the rack because he gathered prestige from the possible confusion. One of the nuns is carrying a wicker basket like the ones that "...Salvation Army babes collect dough with around Christmas time." It inspires Holden to make his ten dollar contribution. This leads to conversation, and that to the discovery that one of the nuns is an English teacher and the other a history teacher. Holden and the English teaching nun have a rather lengthy discussion about books, notably *Romeo and Juliet*. Holden does not like the play because he admires Mercutio and holds Romeo responsible for his death. However, Holden is reticent to discuss the play with a nun: "To tell the truth, it was sort of embarrassing, in a way, to be talking about *Romeo and Juliet* with her. I mean that play gets pretty sexy in some parts, and she was a nun and all...."

Holden has a way of coming back again and again to certain key themes or ideas. In his literary conversation with the nun, he recalls again his earlier remarks about Hardy's *Return of the Native*. He also digresses on the subject of religion. This digression, having to do with Catholicism, recalls earlier discussions of other faiths (see the discussion of Quakers in the preceding chapter). As they part, Holden is guilty of a mild indiscretion; he blows smoke at them. This act causes Holden paroxysms of conscience. The act was ill-mannered. He wonders whether he shouldn't have given them more money. "I apologized like a mad man, and they were very polite about it, but it was very embarrassing anyway....I was sorry anyway, though. Goddam money. It always ends up making you blue as hell."

It is important to note that, little by little, Holden is rejecting all the standard values. One is reminded of a story, "The Door" by E. B. White in which he compares the condition of modern man to the condition of rats in psychological laboratory experiments. His little story uses the experiments of conditioned reflex as a core; rats are trained to jump at a door and rewarded with food when they succeed. Later, the doors are changed and the rats are made neurotic:

...First they would teach you the prayers and the Psalms, and that would be the right door...and the long sweet words with the holy sound, and that would be the one to jump at to get where the food was. Then one day you jumped and it didn't give way, so that all you got was a bump on the nose, and the first bewilderment, the first young bewilderment.

I don't know whether to tell her about the door they substituted or not, he said, the one with the equation on it and the picture of the amoeba reproducing itself by division. Or the one with the photostatic copy of the check for thirty-two dollars and fifty cents. But the jumping was long ago, although the bump is...how those old wounds hurt!...I remember the door with the picture of the girl on it (only it was spring), her arms outstretched in loveliness, her dress...uncaught, beginning the slow, clear, blinding cascade—and I guess we would all like to try that door again, for it seemed like the way and for a while it was the way, the door would open and you would go through winged and exalted (like any rat) and the food would be there, the way the Professor had it arranged, everything O.K., and you had chosen the right door for the world was young. The time they changed that door on me, my nose bled for a hundred hours....

> [*The Second Tree from the Corner,* Harper & Brothers, 1939.]

CHAPTER XVI

Summary

Holden finishes his breakfast around noon. He still has two hours to kill. He walks over to Broadway in the hopes of finding a record shop open because he wants to buy a certain record for his sister Phoebe. He finds a record shop and buys the record. Then he goes to buy tickets for a show to which he can take Sally. Afterwards he goes to Central Park to look for Phoebe, but she is not there. He walks through the park to the American Museum of Natural History, but he does not go in; rather, he takes a taxi to the Biltmore where he is to meet Sally.

Commentary

While walking to Broadway, Holden thinks about the nuns he has met, and compares their humility with that of other persons he knows; with Sally's mother and his own aunt. The nuns come off quite well because they never went to any real expensive ("swanky") place for lunch. This realization makes him feel sorry for the nuns even though he knows that it is not important for nuns to eat in "swanky" places.

Holden next talks about the record that he wants to buy for Phoebe. It is a recording by Estelle Fletcher of "Little Shirley Beans." Holden heard it at school and tried to buy it, but the record is a collector's item. The interpretation is "Dixieland and whorehouse" as opposed to the more likely "cute" interpretation by a white singer. As he walks along, Holden finds himself following a more or less poor family returning from church. The little boy is walking in the gutter, singing to himself. The song he sings is "If a body catch a body coming through the rye." The experience is peculiarly refreshing to Holden: "It made me feel better. It made me feel not so depressed any more." Broadway itself is, however, depressing to Holden.

He can't understand the people lined up and waiting to get in to see a movie. He feels that when a person has nothing else to do, it is all right to go to a movie, but it depresses him to think that all these people are waiting to go to the movie because they *really want* to see the movie. The description of people standing in one of those long, terrible lines, all the way down the block, waiting with this terrific patience for seats and all is certainly evocative. Georges Duhamel, in his book *America the Menace,* writes the following description of just such a line:

> Indeed all these people paid very dearly for their favorite pleasure and for the right to await, in clusters along the wall, under a sooty drizzle, their admittance to the sanctuary of the movies, the temple wherein the images move. Thus aligned they hardly spoke, but stood patiently, with vague eyes, already submissive to the hypnosis that soon would seize them in the enchanted darkness. From time to time a portion of the queue was ingested into the lower orifices of the building; the line shuffled along, sprouted, lengthened. Within the cavern the pilgrim presented his obolus, his dollar.

Duhamel presents the scene as a visit to hell. He concludes his study of the American movie with the observation that "...a people stupefied by the fugitive, epidermal pleasures of the movie, obtained without the slightest intellectual or aesthetic effort, will one day find itself incapable of any sustained endeavor, a protoplasmic mass unequal to any disciplined mental activity."

Holden finds his record and buys it, for five dollars, and then he again decides to phone Jane Gallagher. This time he actually does call, but her mother answers and Holden hangs up. He is still not in the mood. Then he goes to buy theater tickets. Relatively few plays are available. He buys two orchestra tickets to *I Know My Love,* with the Lunts, because he knows that Sally admires them. Holden does not. In fact, he doesn't like theater, and he doesn't like actors.

Plays are not as bad as movies, he feels, but they are not good, and actors never behave like people. A relatively long digression discusses theater in general, and even Sir Laurence Olivier and *Hamlet* come in for negative criticism. Holden feels that Olivier presented Hamlet "too much like a goddam general, instead of a sad, screwed-up type guy."

Having acquired the tickets, Holden goes to Central Park to look for his sister Phoebe on the chance that she might be playing there. The park is relatively deserted, but Holden has a series of encounters with children. First he meets a little girl about his sister's age and asks her if she knows Phoebe. They have a brief conversation, and Holden helps her tighten her skates. "God, I love it when a kid's nice and polite when you tighten their skate for them or something. Most kids are. They really are." Later he sees two little children playing on a seesaw. He helps the lighter child, but feels he is not really wanted.

Between these two encounters he is walking toward the American Museum of Natural History. He thinks about his trips to the museum as a schoolboy. He points out the permanence of certain of the displays as opposed to the constantly changing nature of human beings and thinks of himself and his sister in relation to change and permanence.

When he finally gets to the museum, Holden simply does not feel like going in. Instead he takes a taxi to the Biltmore Hotel to meet Sally.

CHAPTER XVII

Summary
This chapter recounts the events of the date Holden had with Sally. They meet at the Biltmore, go to the theater, and afterwards to Radio City to ice skate. They have an argument, and Sally goes home angry.

Commentary

The events of this chapter are told very sketchily, but the digressions are many and long. Holden is early for the date. He spends his time sightseeing — that is, looking at all the other people, particularly the girls, waiting for other people. He speculates about girls and about bores. He is depressed by the idea that most of the "swell-looking girls" were going to marry bores, but then he confesses that he doesn't understand bores. He thinks about a boy named Harris Macklin with whom he roomed at Elkton Hills. Macklin was a bore, but he whistled beautifully. He adds, however, that he doesn't know much about bores. He even suggests that we shouldn't feel sorry for a girl who is married to a bore because maybe all bores have some secret talent: "maybe they're secretly all terrific whistlers or something." This attitude is akin to the basic attitudes of Zen Buddhism.

Finally, Sally arrives. She looks very attractive and Holden says that he felt like marrying her the moment he saw her. Several times during this chapter he will say that he is crazy. He says it here for the first time. "I'm crazy. I didn't even like her much, and yet all of a sudden I felt like I was in love with her and wanted to marry her. I swear to God I'm crazy. I admit it." Together they take a taxi to the theater. Conversation is small talk. In the taxi, they "neck" a bit, because Holden is being "seductive as hell." Again, Holden repeats that he is crazy. "Then, just to show you how crazy I am, when we were coming out of this big clinch, I told her I loved her and all. It was a lie, of course, but the thing is, I *meant* it when I said it. I'm crazy. I swear to God I am."

A fairly long section is devoted to the performance itself. The play is not bad, but Holden cannot get much interested. He enjoys the Lunts' performances, but claims that they are *too* good, and specifically recalls his comments about Ernie in the Village club. During the intermission Holden and Sally go out into the lobby to smoke. Holden engages in some people-watching. Sally sees a boy whom she knows slightly, a George something-or-other who goes to Andover, and Holden is subjected to another "phony" conversation. The conversation is continued during the second intermission and after the performance, and Holden is very annoyed. By the time they finally escape from George, Holden is ready to take Sally home, but she suggests that they go ice skating at Radio City. Her real motive comes out shortly: "You can rent those darling skating skirts...Jeanette Cultz did it last week." In any case, they go. Holden observes that Sally does look quite good in the skirt. But, unfortunately, neither of them are good skaters, and Holden soon suggests that they get a table in the adjoining bar and Sally quickly agrees. The waiter will not serve Holden alcohol, so both drink Coca Cola. Holden compensates for his nervousness by lighting matches and letting them burn down to the end. He admits that "It's a nervous habit." Sally wants to know whether or not Holden will come to her house to help her trim the Christmas tree on Christmas Eve. She is uncomfortable because her ankles hurt from skating. Suddenly Holden begins a serious conversation. Holden pours out all his disappointment. He tells her that he hates school, hates New York. Sally is not terribly interested in the conversation and wishes he would change the subject. She tells him not to shout, but Holden is working himself up. Suddenly he proposes a retreat, out of the city, into the woods. As he talks he gets more excited. He proposes marriage and an idyllic natural life in the woods. Sally thinks the idea is fantastic; her approach to the problem is a safe, middle-class approach. She tells him that after he finishes college and accomplishes the standard goals then there will be time. Holden becomes impatient and depressed again. His excitement and enthusiasm vanish, and he is left only with an emotional hangover. Sally does not understand what he is talking about, and he is sorry that he tried to have "an intelligent conversation" with her. He tells Sally that he wants to leave because she is giving him a "royal pain in the ass." Sally becomes infuriated, and Holden admits that he probably shouldn't have said what he did, "but she was depressing the hell" out of him.

That marks the end of the date and the conversation. Sally leaves in a huff, justifiably. She will not even accept Holden's quite sincere apologies. The absurdity of the whole situation strikes Holden funny, and he commits the grand *faux pas* by laughing. Alone, Holden speculates about his role in the scene. He doesn't even know why he proposed to Sally. He realizes that he doesn't like her very much and wouldn't get along with her, but the thing he doesn't understand is that at the time of the proposal, he meant it. He concludes that he must be a madman. But Holden's suggested retreat is actually paralleled in Salinger's life, and he does live in the sort of naturally ideal situation, in New Hampshire, for which Holden seems to hunger. But Holden perhaps confuses tenderness and loneliness with love, a common emotional error.

CHAPTER XVIII

Summary

After he leaves Sally, Holden gets a sandwich. Then he tries to call Jane Gallagher again but no one answers. Instead, in desperation, he calls Carl Luce, an older boy he knew at Whooton School, and makes an appointment to meet him at ten o'clock. Then, to kill time, he goes to Radio City Music Hall to a movie.

Commentary

Holden is not sufficiently affected by his scene with Sally for it to affect his appetite. He has "a Swiss cheese sandwich and a malted," and then he tries to call Jane again, but Jane is unattainable. He digresses to explain that he doesn't understand women, or rather girls. His conclusion is that if girls "...like a boy, no matter how big a bastard he is, they'll say he has an inferiority complex, and if they *don't* like him, no matter how nice a guy he is, or how big an inferiority complex he has, they'll say he's conceited. Even smart girls do it."

Simply to have something to do, Holden calls Carl Luce. Holden does not like him particularly but he is intelligent and Holden feels the need of intellectual conversation. Luce cannot dine with Holden, but he agrees to meet him for a drink at ten o'clock. Since he has quite a bit of time to kill, Holden goes to Radio City. The bulk of the chapter is devoted to his comments about the stage show and the movie. The stage show consists in part of a special Christmas presentation, which Holden finds "phony." Like George Duhamel, Holden cannot accept the pseudo-religious qualities. Duhamel writes: "The 'feature' was followed by vaudeville and a series of 'shorts.' The great organ uttered vaguely religious sonorities, for the cinema replaces and abridges all other institutions." The plot of the movie, recounted in detail, is sentimental and artificial. Holden's summary comment is: "All I can say is, don't see it if you don't want to puke all over yourself."

Another digression takes up the case of a fellow watcher, a woman who weeps throughout the film. Holden observes the woman and makes some wry comments about human nature. The film was completely phony, but the way the woman was weeping, a person would think that she was a fine and kindhearted woman. But she wasn't. She had a little boy with her who wanted to go to the bathroom, but she refused to take him. Holden can't understand how a woman can cry over a phony film and still be such "bastards at heart." Holden has discovered an important truth of human nature; that people are more likely to be concerned over the imaginary ills of imaginary people than over the real ills immediately obvious to them — thus the enormous success of the "soap-opera."

When the movie is over, Holden starts walking to the bar where he is to meet Carl Luce. On the way he thinks about war and the army, thoughts produced by the subject matter of the movie. His brother D. B. was in the army and in the war, and Holden uses him as an example. He believes that D. B. hated the army more than he hated the war, and Holden talks about his own intolerance of standardization and discipline. He is a philosophical conscientious objector, quite willing to be shot, but not willing to serve in the army. D. B. convinced him to read *A Farewell to Arms,* but he does not like the novel, nor does he understand how the same person could enjoy that and *The Great Gatsby* or an unnamed book by Ring Lardner at the same time. The latter works are in his opinion good while the Hemingway novel is "phony."

CHAPTER XIX

Summary

Holden meets Carl Luce at the Wicker Bar, and they have a couple of drinks together. The conversation is largely about sex.

Commentary

Holden arrives at the bar early. He is able to get served, and he spends his time people-watching. He discovers some "flits" at one end of the bar, and the man next to him is trying to "snow hell out of the babe he was with." Holden describes the bar as a place where "phonies" gather to be very sophisticated. He discusses the floor show, two girls named Tina and Janine, who sang off-color songs in French and English. "If you sat around there long enough and heard all the phonies applauding and all, you got to hate everybody in the world..." Even the bartender is a toady.

Luce finally arrives. They sit at a table and have a few drinks together. Luce had been Holden's student advisor at school, but it had been his custom to hold sex lectures for the younger boys late at night. His father is a psychologist, and Luce seems to believe that most people are sexual perverts of one sort or another. The conversation at the bar is largely of sexual matters. Luce presently has a Chinese mistress about thirty years old, a sculptress, and Holden is tremendously impressed and curious. He tries to pry, but Luce doesn't want to talk about it. Holden tells Luce how "lousy" sex is for him and explains that he can't get excited over a girl unless he likes her a lot. "It really screws up my sex life something awful." What Holden needs, according to Luce, is psychoanalysis. He needs to "recognize the patterns" of his mind. Then Luce has to leave. Holden asks him if he has been analyzed by his father, and Luce admits that, although massive analysis was not necessary, his father did help him to adjust himself. Holden begs him to stay, frankly admitting that he is terribly lonesome, but Luce has to go. Holden has appealed for help to another source, and again he has been rejected. Luce is in no position to help anyone. He has his own problems. Even if he were willing to help, even if he recognized Holden's need, he would be unable to help. Little by little, Holden is being forced into a corner. Help is simply not available.

CHAPTER XX

Summary
    After Luce leaves, Holden remains in the Wicker Bar and continues drinking. Ultimately he gets rather drunk. He goes to the washroom and soaks his head to sober up. Then he leaves the bar and goes to Central Park to see for himself whether or not the ducks are still there. Finally, believing that he is going to catch pneumonia and die, he decides to go home to see his sister. He walks from the Park to the apartment house where his family lives.

Commentary
    It is now very late Sunday night, some thirty hours since the beginning of the story. Holden is on the downward slide, and events will occur rapidly now. Holden remains in the Wicker Bar after Luce leaves, Partially at least because he has no place to go. His bags are checked at Grand Central Station. He does not even have a hotel room, and his money is quite depleted. Later in the chapter, he counts his money and discovers that he has only four dollars and thirty cents left. He drinks some more at the bar, and apparently he gets quite drunk—at least he reports several times that he was very drunk. He waits for Tina and Janine to do their act, but they have been replaced by a new act, a singer named Valencia. Holden "gave her the old eye" while she was performing, but she apparently found it possible to resist him, and she left right after her performance. Disappointed with these developments, Holden decides again to call Jane Gallagher. He goes to the phone booth, but suddenly decides that he is really not in the mood. Instead he calls Sally Hayes and again promises her that he will come and help her trim her tree on Christmas Eve. At the same time, he is again imagining himself a tough guy. He tells Sally that Rock's mob got him, and he makes believe that he has a bullet in his stomach. Sally appears to have forgiven him for the events of the afternoon, but she does tell him to go get some sleep, and she does finally hang up on him. After all, it is after one o'clock in the morning. Holden remains in the

phone booth, hanging on to the telephone to keep from fainting. Then he goes to the men's room and soaks his head in the wash-bowl. He does not dry himself, but sits on a radiator with water streaming down his shirt. Apparently he remains there quite a while. "I didn't have anything else to do, so I kept sitting on the radiator and counting these little white squares on the floor." Ultimately, Valencia's accompanyist comes in to comb his hair. Holden talks to him, but the pianist is not interested. He simply urges Holden to go home, then he "just went out. He was all through combing his hair and patting it and all, so he left."

Holden finally leaves the washroom and starts to leave the bar. He runs into a small problem at the hat check room, because he has lost his check, but the girl there helps him and finally sends him on his way. Outside, Holden cannot decide where to go. Finally he decides to go to Central Park to see for himself what happens to to the ducks in the lake. Because of the darkness and his condition, he has some difficulty in finding the lake, but he does find it, and he walks completely around it looking for the ducks. He does not find them, and this question remains an unsolved one. He sits on a bench and counts his money. The water in his hair has frozen and he is very cold. He begins to worry about catching pneumonia and dying. Then he digresses to think about Allie in his grave. He describes a visit to Allie's grave. During the visit, it began to rain. All the other visitors ran for the protection of their cars, but Holden was de-pressed because Allie had to lie there in his grave and let the rain fall on him. As he sees the other visitors leaving, Holden thinks how they can go some place for a nice dinner, but Allie has to stay there in his grave; it almost drove him crazy. "I just wish he wasn't there. You didn't know him. If you'd known him, you'd know what I mean." It is important to remember that these comments are addressed to the psychoanalyst in the rest home.

In any case, he is convinced that he himself will die of pneu-monia. To take his mind off his potential death, he goes down to the lake and skips his change across the water, but the diversion does not help. Finally, he decides to go to see his sister before he dies. Now, a few chapters ago he was quite willing to die rather than go into the army. But with death more real and immediate instead of remote and theoretical, his attitude changes. He walks home from the park. His return home is inevitable. He has been circling it like a moth circling a candle flame. His sense of guilt over his expulsion from school, and his fear of his parents' reaction have kept him away. But his need has drawn him, and his need is greater than his fear and guilt.

CHAPTER XXI

Summary

Holden arrives at the apartment. A substitute elevator boy does not recognize him, so he is able to achieve secrecy. He lets himself in and very quietly makes his way to his sister's room. She isn't there. She likes to sleep in D. B.'s room when he is away, so Holden goes there. She is asleep, and Holden wanders about the room, touching objects, looking at her books, reimmersing himself in Phoebe's character. Finally he wakes her up. At first she is delighted to see him, and she talks excitedly about small things in her life. But shortly she guesses that he has been expelled again, and she puts her pillow over her head and refuses to talk to him.

Commentary

This chapter and the next one form the emotional center of the book. In this chapter Holden faces his most serious disappointment. Throughout the book he has been thinking about Phoebe. She is, apparently, the only person who understands him — or at least this is what he believes. He has been going to see her ever since he left school. His odyssey is almost ended. Phoebe's understanding and compassion are what Holden has been seeking.

The elevator operator at the house is a substitute, and Holden lies to him and confuses him to maintain secrecy. He lets himself into the apartment, quietly, to avoid discovery by his parents. He creeps to Phoebe's room only to find that she is not there. She sleeps in D. B.'s room when he is away. He must make one more perilous trip. Finally, he arrives where she is. She is sleeping, and Holden turns on the light and wanders about the room, looking at familiar objects, touching her things; he sits on the desk and reads her books. Slowly he reëstablishes contact with her through inanimate objects. "I went around the room, very quiet and all, looking at stuff for a while. I felt swell, for a change. I didn't even feel like I was getting pneumonia or anything anymore. I just felt good, for a change." He talks about Phoebe, about her neatness, her habits, her attitudes, her intelligence. There is wonder and awe in his reverence for her. Finally he wakes her.

At first, she is delighted to see him. She puts her arms about him. She babbles childishly about a movie she has seen. She also tells him, incidentally, that his parents are out for the evening — thus his caution was unnecessary. She talks about a play she is going to be in. She fills him in on family events. He tells her about the record he bought for her, which he dropped in his last visit to Central Park when he was drunk. He gives her the pieces of the record, which she takes and cherishes. But in the midst of the glad reunion, she guesses that he has been expelled from school again. Her comment is "Daddy'll *kill* you." Her disappointment is obvious; she hits him. At last, she puts her pillow over her head and she will not talk to him. She rejects him. This is the cruelest rejection of all. Holden tries to tease her out of it, but she is adamant. Finally, Holden leaves briefly to look for more cigarettes. This is the third climax.

CHAPTER XXII

Summary

The interview with Phoebe continues. She relents and talks to Holden. Holden tries to explain his failure. She challenges him to name anything he likes and to tell her what he would like to be. He tells her that he wants to be the catcher in the rye. Finally, he decides to call Mr. Antolini.

Commentary

Little by little, Holden is able to awaken Phoebe's compassion instead of her rejection. Phoebe has a much greater sense of reality than Holden has. At first, when she permits herself to talk to him again, the conversation is minor. But then she asks him why he failed again. Holden's anguished cry points up the suffering he has undergone. "Oh, God, Phoebe, don't ask me. I'm sick of everybody asking me that....A million reasons why." It is interesting that, except for Mr. Spencer, no one in the course of the story has asked him. But the obvious implication is that he has asked himself a million times. Then he tries to explain. The reasons are real enough, but not exceptional. The reasons have all been explicitly demonstrated throughout the book. The reasons are the harshness, stupidity, and brutality not only of school life, but of life in general. In the early chapters it was Ackley and Stradlater who represented the evils of life. In later chapters Maurice was added to the list. These are the major symbols, but the waiters, taxi drivers, hotel occupants, club entertainers and patrons, fellow students (male and female) are all in these same categories to one degree or another. The anquished outpouring continues to a second outcry: "God, Phoebe! I can't explain. I just didn't like anything that was *happening* at Pencey. I can't explain."

Phoebe's observation, "You don't like *any*thing that's happening" interrupts the mounting wave of protest and turns it aside. Holden starts to explain what he does like. He finds himself thinking about the two nuns he met and about a boy at Elkton who chose to die rather than to allow himself to be brutalized and made a moral coward and a liar by the other boys. Phoebe calls him back again by demanding that he *name* things he likes. Holden replies "I like Allie...And I like doing what I'm doing right now. Sitting here with you, and talking, and thinking about stuff, and—," but this does not satisfy Phoebe. Allie *is* dead, and sitting and talking isn't real. She asks him what he wants to be—a scientist, or a lawyer. He rejects both—science because he is not good at it, and law for a very complex reason. A lawyer is "phony," either in the sense that he is a "solid citizen," or in the sense that, like Ernie and the Lunts, he can become so good that he doesn't know when he is sincere and when he is merely seeking approval. Suddenly, Holden knows what he wants to be. He wants to be the catcher in the rye. His vision is based on a faulty reading of Burns: "If a body *catch* a body coming through the rye." It is a completely unrealistic vision. Holden has a dream in which many young children are playing in a big field. Every time one of the kids comes close to the edge of the cliff, Holden is there to keep him from falling off. "That's all I'd do all day, I'd just be the catcher in the rye and all." Holden suffers simply from the way things are in a world in which love is not sufficiently distributed. He wants to be a professional "lover," but not in the traditional sense. He will be a fielder of children because they love more easily — they have not yet learned to withhold love. (And the act of fielding children should recall Allie's fielder's glove with the love poems in green ink.) Holden is called upon to make judgments. To explain. So far he has been able to make judgments. He has condemned Stradlater and Maurice with his hatred, but his personal value system is based upon love and such judgments are harder to make. He now must make one more quest for understanding. He calls Mr. Antolini.

CHAPTER XXIII

Summary

Holden convinces Mr. Antolini that he must see him. The conversation on the phone is brief because Holden is afraid his parents will come in. They do not and Holden returns to Phoebe. They dance together. Their parents return, and Holden hides in the closet. Phoebe lies to protect him, and their parents go to bed not knowing that he is there. Phoebe lends him some money, and he slips out of the apartment.

Commentary

This scene is a continuation of the sparkling Holden-Phoebe relationship. The dancing together is absurd under the circumstances, but it illustrates the rapport that exists between these two. Phoebe has compassion and love and she wants to help Holden, but she *is* still a child. When their parents return, she freely lies to protect Holden, even to the point of admitting that she had smoked a cigarette. She gladly gives Holden her Christmas money, every penny of it. Her compassion and love are so freely given and so much in contrast to all other events described in the book that Holden weeps, almost becomes hysterical. Finally, he leaves the apartment to go to see Mr. Antolini. He is far less cautious leaving, because he no longer fears being caught; in fact, he almost wishes that his parents would catch him, but he successfully completes his escape.

CHAPTER XXIV

Summary

Holden arrives at the Antolini apartment. A brief digression indicates that Antolini was Holden's English teacher at Elkton Hills School, that he was not married then, but that he married a woman older than himself who has a great deal of money, and that he presently teaches at N.Y.U. Mrs. Antolini makes coffee, and Holden and Mr. Antolini talk while Mrs. Antolini goes off to bed. They talk for some time, but Holden finds it hard to concentrate because he is very tired and not feeling terribly well. Finally Mr. Antolini makes up the bed for Holden and he goes to sleep. He awakens some time later to find Mr. Antolini sitting on the floor next to him patting his head. Holden is frightened, and as quickly as he can, he leaves.

Commentary

Holden goes to see Mr. Antolini at this point in his progress because Antolini represents for him a fortress of moral-conscience. Several times in preceding chapters, Holden has remarked about Antolini's intellect, and about the fact that he was the best teacher Holden had ever had. When he arrives at Antolini's house, Holden finds him quite drunk. The fact that Antolini is married to a woman much older than himself whom he obviously does not love also bothers Holden. Holden wants to sleep — he is exhausted and not at all well — but Antolini wants to talk. To a large extent his analysis of Holden's state of mind is accurate enough, and his advice is good, but Holden is not in a condition to entirely understand or appreciate what is being said to him. Holden is bored with him and disappointed too. His disappointment turns to active revulsion when Antolini performs an action which Holden interprets as perverted. Holden is terrified of the implications as well as revolted, and he runs away.

As far as Antolini's approach to Holden's problem is concerned, it is too academic. Holden needs practical help, compassion, understanding, but Antolini offers him theory, philosophy, and the wrong kind of love. The last idol turns out to have feet of clay like all the others. But there is a significant difference to Holden's response, reflected in the following chapter. He still runs away as he has before, but his retrospective attitude is different. When he runs away, he is ready to condemn Antolini. He changes his mind.

CHAPTER XXV

Summary

It is Monday morning, just getting light, about forty hours since the beginning of the story. Holden returns to Grand Central Station and sleeps in the waiting room. He awakens about nine o'clock Monday and starts thinking about the events of the previous night. To stop his thinking, Holden picks up a magazine, left behind by some transient, and reads it. Then he goes out for a walk. He watches some men unload a large Christmas tree, then goes to a restaurant and has some coffee. He is not feeling well at all. He walks along 5th Avenue. As he walks he begins having the illusion that he will disappear. He talks to Allie. Again he walks to Central Park. There he sits for about an hour and decides that he will go away—out West. He decides to see Phoebe once more before he goes, and he goes to her school to get a note to her telling her where and when to meet him. In the school, Holden finds profanity written on the walls and rubs it out. He delivers his note to the principal's office. Then he walks over to the Metropolitan Museum of Art to wait for Phoebe. He encounters two small boys and helps them to find the display of Egyptian mummies. Holden is now suffering from diarrhea and goes to the rest room. There he faints, but when he recovers he feels somewhat better. He goes out to the main door to wait for Phoebe. She is late. When she does arrive she is carrying a suitcase. She has decided to go with Holden. Holden tells her that she cannot go and they quarrel. Holden tells her that she must go back to school, but she refuses. He promises not to go away. He checks her bag at the museum and they walk into the zoo in the park together. Little by little as they walk, Phoebe's anger dissipates and she finally forgives him completely. They walk through the zoo and end up at the carrousel where the action of the novel ends.

Commentary

This is a very long chapter in which several lines of action are brought to a culmination. First, Holden reconsiders the events at Mr. Antolini's house. There is an important difference in this reconsideration. "...I wondered if just maybe I was wrong about thinking he was making a flitty pass at me. I wondered if maybe he just liked to pat guys on the head when they're asleep. I mean how can you tell about that stuff for sure? You can't." In effect, Holden has refused to judge Antolini. Having abandoned the outlet of condemnation, only greater frustration is left for Holden. He justifies his unwillingness to judge Antolini by retelling again the story of the suicide of James Castle. It was Antolini who "...finally picked up that boy that jumped out of the window...He didn't even give a damn if his coat got all bloody." This is a moral judgment which Holden made earlier. He cannot now refute that judgment. Antolini has moral value.

Holden's unwillingness to judge is a sign of growth. But his own personality reasserts itself. He reads a magazine article and decides that he has cancer and is going to die. To escape his thoughts, he goes for a walk again, and again is drawn to the park. As he walks along he begins to have delusions. The delusions belong to the syndrome of schizophrenia. He talks to Allie, his patron saint, as he walks along, begging Allie to keep him from disappearing. When he gets to the park, he sits down to rest, for about an hour. He decides to go away, out West, and to live close to nature. He decides to pretend that he is a deaf-mute so that he will minimize his contact with people. He decides to see Phoebe once more before he goes away, and to return her Christmas money. He goes to her school to get a note delivered to her asking her to meet him at the Museum of Modern Art at noon. At the school he finds profanity written on the wall. "It drove me damn near crazy. I thought how Phoebe and all the other little kids would see it, and how they'd wonder what the hell it meant, and then finally some dirty kid would tell them—all cockeyed, naturally—what it meant, and how they'd all *think* about it and maybe even *worry* about it for a couple of days." He imagines how he would kill the person who wrote it. And then, fearing that he will be caught and thought to have written it himself, he rubs it out. He is fielding little children on the brink of evil — this catcher in the rye. He delivers his note to the principal's office and sees it on its way to Phoebe. Then he chats with the elderly woman in the office, telling her that he too had attended that school. When he leaves, she calls "good luck" after him, recalling Spencer. "God, how I hate it when somebody yells 'Good Luck!' at me when I'm leaving somewhere. It's depressing." Going down the staircase, he finds another profane remark, this time cut into the wall with a knife. "It wouldn't come off. It's hopeless anyway. If you had a million years to do it in, you couldn't rub out even *half* the...signs in the world. It's impossible."

It is twenty minutes to twelve, and Holden goes to the museum to wait for Phoebe. He encounters two little boys playing hooky, and spends some time with them helping them to locate the display of Egyptian mummies and the reconstruction of a tomb. The children become frightened and run away, but Holden stays in the tomb, enjoying the peace and quiet until he discovers another sign, even there. He feels ill again and goes to the bathroom. He has diarrhea, and then faints. The fainting makes him feel better and he goes out to the main door to wait for Phoebe. While he is waiting, he daydreams again about his ideal home in the west. He plans to allow his sister and brother to visit him there, but he will have a rule for behavior in his forest cabin: "...that nobody could do anything phony when they visited me."

Suddenly he realizes that it is twenty-five to one and Phoebe has not arrived. He begins to fear that she didn't get his note. He really wants to see her. At last she appears, carrying a big suitcase and announces that she is going with him. Partially as a result of his shock at her announcement, and partially as a result of his illness, he is brutal to her in his prohibition. They have an argument and Phoebe becomes very angry with him. She refuses to return to school. Together, they set off for the zoo in the park, at first walking on opposite sides of the street, but, coming closer and closer together as they go along, until finally Phoebe forgives him completely. They finish at the carrousel. Holden buys Phoebe a ticket and sits in the rain watching her go around. Suddenly, Holden feels happy and contented watching Phoebe ride the carrousel. "I was damn near bawling, I felt so damn happy." He doesn't know why he felt so happy, but it was just a feeling of perfect freedom. Holden is no longer capable of assigning an absolute value to anything. This is completely consistent with the change indicated in response to the Antolini incident.

Holden is quite sick, but he is willing to return home at once. In a sense he has been beaten by the system. He suffers from the world as it is. Most men learn to suppress the occasional invading idea that the world as it is really cannot be borne, but a few — children, maniacs, and saints — never learn the trick.

CHAPTER XXVI

Summary
Holden is talking directly to the analyst in the rest home in California. He predicts that he will be out soon and that he will go back to school next September.

Commentary
Obviously the circumstances narrated by Holden in the bulk of this novel have resulted in what is politely called a "rest cure" for Holden. But even after the questions and the treatment Holden still does not know the answers and still suffers from lack of love. In answer to D. B.'s questions about his story, Holden explains that he doesn't know what the truth is any more. All that he knows is that he now misses most of the people he has talked about. "It's funny. Don't ever tell anybody anything. If you do, you start missing everybody." This chapter serves to complete the cycle of the book. Its opening and closing chapters serve as a frame within which the story takes place. The story itself, as has been illustrated, is divided into four developments, separated at the seventh, fourteenth and twenty-first chapters at which points the structural climaxes occur. The last

chapter has the essential function of closing the frame. Most of the narrative details are completed in the preceding chapter. In a sense, in terms of the story, the last chapter is an anticlimax, but it is structurally necessary. As part of the narrative, it seems to need little commentary, for its point is really quite apparent.

A NOTE ON HOLDEN IN RELATION
TO THE SALINGER CANON

Catcher in the Rye is Salinger's only novel to date, but it is not his only work, and in a sense Salinger's work must be considered more or less as a unity. Holden Caulfield is cut from the same piece of cloth as most of the members of the Glass family and as Sergeant X of the war stories. The Salinger hero is a special kind of person and deserves special consideration.

All of Salinger's protagonists, since it is really hard to call them heroes, are in a sense young, mad saints, or perhaps, mad, saintly youths; that is, they are not so much in rebellion against the established world of adult middle-class values as they are per-haps victims of that world. They are all hypersensitive individuals who suffer from excesses of beauty as they do from failures of love. Seymour Glass, who occurs in a relatively large number of stories, is perhaps the best spokesman for the whole group. "I have scars on my hands from touching certain people...Certain heads, certain colors, and textures of human hair leave permanent marks on me. Other things too. Charlotte once ran away from me outside the studio, and I grabbed her dress to stop her, to keep her near me. A yellow cotton dress I loved because it was too long for her. I still have a lemon-yellow mark on the palm of my right hand." There are certain things, unnoticed by most people, which consti-tute orgasms of beauty to the Salinger protagonists. With Holden it was the fact that Jane Gallagher kept all her kings in the back row when she played checkers, or it was Phoebe riding the carrousel in the rain in Central Park. At the same time, they are victims of the society, being eroded by the lack of love. Holden is a refugee from respectability. He is possessed of a strong sense of justice and a personal morality which is a-Christian. (He is sure, for example, that Jesus could not have sent Judas to Hell.) His moral system and his sense of justice force him to detect horrifying flaws in the society in which he lives. For Holden, all these flaws are summed up in the one word "phony."

Salinger's most significant creation, outside of Holden himself, is the Glass family, and Seymour is the dominating force in that family. Seymour's suicide is recorded in an early story, "A Great Day for Bananafish," but it is explained only in subsequent stories: "Franny," *"Raise High the Roof-Beam, Carpenters,"* "Zooey," and "Seymour: An Introduction," all of which appeared first in *The New Yorker* magazine before 1955 and 1959 and have been subsequently reissued as books. In that first story, however, much of the explanation of Salinger's work lies. Just prior to his suicide, Seymour spends an interlude with a little girl on the beach in Miami. The little girl is a complete unknown, just a child playing on the beach. He talks to her about bananafish. Shortly after this conversation, Seymour returns to his hotel suite and commits suicide. The impression of the story is that he is driven to his desperate act by the stupidity and insensitivity of his wife and his mother-in-law, but the later story *"Raise High the Roof-Beam, Carpenters,"* clearly shows that if they are insensitive and stupid, they are at least without malice. (Holden says: "...I don't know about bores....They don't hurt anybody, most of them, and maybe they're secretly all terrific whistlers or something.") They are not responsible for Seymour's state. Rather, Seymour is a bananafish; he is so stuffed with sensation that he is trapped in a hole and can no longer swim in society. Seymour has banana fever. Holden has banana fever too, and knowing that he has it and what it is helps to understand why Holden acts as he does and why he is driven to the verge of insanity. Holden also has scars from contact with beauty and other scars from contact with the "phony." Holden's principal difficulty is not that he is a rebel, nor that he hates the society and its mores, nor that he is a coward, but rather that he is unable to sort out, or to purge himself of his burden of sensation. He is bloated with memory and experience, and Salinger indicates this in the intentional confusion of time in his thoughts, so that Allie's death, experiences at Pencey, Whooton, and Elkton Hills, prior dates, and immediate events are all mixed together and are not separated by time levels, not even in verb tense. The novel ends with Holden's confession that he misses everybody. He remembers good things like Allie and Jane Gallagher with equal intensity with bad things like Maurice and the profanity on the school wall, so that ultimately all distinctions between good and bad disappear. All experiences become merely a part of himself. He says: "Don't ever tell anybody anything. If you do, you start missing everybody."

Thus, Holden is inexorably burdened with sheer experience. This situation is unbearable, but the unbearable aspect of it is not that things are either good or bad, but rather that experience itself is passing away. Holden wants to retain everything. In thinking about his visits to the American Museum of Natural History, Holden believes certain things "should stay the way they are. You ought to be able to stick them in one of those big glass cases and just leave them alone." His image of himself as a catcher in the rye is in keeping with his general attitude as well, since he wishes to catch experience and keep it from dropping out of sight just as he wants to save the children from falling over the cliff. And experience is always young, so children are the perfect image for it. As he makes no distinction between good and bad children in his catching, so he makes no distinction between good and bad, important and unimportant, valid and invalid experience. As he saves all children, so he saves all experience. Since he is unable in any reasonable way to purge himself of experience, the only possible salvation is suicide. Holden contemplates it at least once in the story. After the incident with Maurice and the prostitute, Holden "felt like jumping out the window. I probably would've done it too, if I'd been sure somebody'd cover me up as soon as I landed."

More generally, though, the whole sequence of experiences narrated in the novel indicates a seeking after destruction. There are constant references to it. The death of James Castle, Phoebe's repetition of the expression "Daddy'll *kill* you," Holden's own daydreams of having a bullet in his guts, of dying of cancer, Holden's concern for the ducks in Central Park, all of these express the death wish to a certain extent.

Going back for a moment to the key story "A Perfect Day for Bananafish," the title is interesting. It is a *perfect* day for bananafish on the day that Seymour kills himself. Obviously, it is a perfect day because the bananafish can only end his suffering by dying, and the surest way of dying is to kill oneself. But the difference between Holden and Seymour here is significant. Seymour can do it, and Holden cannot. Age, experience, degree of saturation, intensity of experience are all factors in the significant difference. But probably the most significant point lies in the fact that Seymour is articulate and Holden is not.

Many of Salinger's other stories are explorations of this same problem, but with various solutions. In the earlier stories, the war serves as the cause of what can generally be called banana fever, and at the same time, the war stands in the way of clear solutions. In such stories as "For Esmé — With Love and Squalor," as well as the other group of war stories, the war itself is both cause and effect. It is only with the publication of *Catcher in the Rye* that the true diagnosis of banana fever occurs.

QUESTIONS

1. Several times, there appear to be discrepancies between what Holden does and what he says. For example, in Chapter XII Holden says, "I can drink all night and not even show it," but in Chapter XX Holden gets very drunk — "Boy, was I drunk"; several times. Holden calls attention to his suavity, but his conversations with women are not terribly suave. Are these illustrations lapses in memory in Salinger, or do they serve some function in the novel?

2. Right from the beginning of the novel, Holden employs the word "phony" to describe the behavior of a number of people — Mr. Spencer, Ossenburger, even his own father. Can Holden's use of the word be specifically defined or is it so loose as to have no meaning?

3. Is Pencey Prep (or Elkton Hills or Whooton School) intended as a symbol of twentieth-century American culture?

4. What are the functions of Allie, Phoebe, and Jane Gallagher in the book?

5. What is Holden's attitude toward religion?

6. What is Holden's attitude toward accepted morality?

7. What do Ernie, the piano player, the Lunts, Lawrence Olivier, and lawyers all have in common? What significance do these common factors have in the context of the novel?

8. Holden makes aesthetic judgments about several books. He seems to like Thomas Hardy. On the basis of the evidence in the novel, how can his admiration for Hardy be justified?

   On the same evidence, how can his dislike of Hemingway be justified?

9. Is the novel essentially comic or tragic, or is some other term necessary to define it?

10. What is the significance of children in the novel?

SUGGESTED THEME TOPICS

1. Discuss the unity of the novel as a whole.

2. Discuss the significance of Chapters VII, XIV, and XXI as focal units in the structure of the book.

3. Discuss Salinger's use of verb tense to indicate shifts in time level in Holden's thinking.

4. Discuss Holden's red hat as a functional symbol in the novel.

5. Discuss Allie as a symbolic figure in the novel.

6. Holden makes it quite clear that he considers certain things "phony," and that he rejects these things, but what does Holden offer as a substitute for the things he rejects?

7. Is Salinger's treatment of children essentially "sentimental"?

8. The critic George Steiner has written: "Salinger flatters the very ignorance and moral shallowness of his young readers." Attack or defend this point of view.

9. What exactly is it that brings Holden to the "rest home" in California? Does he belong there or is he as sane as anyone else?

10. Holden's rejections of certain things imply that society is wrong and he is right. This attitude seems to indicate a superiority complex. Does Holden feel superior to other people? Is Holden actually superior to other people?

11. Holden is a person who, for whatever reasons, is removed from society and therefore more independent than the person who must rely upon society. In this sense he is similar to many other characters in American literature — that is, he belongs to the tradition of the American Adam, the man who wishes to live alone in the wilderness. Compare Holden's isolation with the isolation of as many other characters from American literature as you think fit in the tradition.

12. Are the incidents in *Catcher in the Rye* arranged in the best possible order? Do they build logically from one to another? For example, could Holden's long scene with Phoebe have come after his interview with Mr. Antolini as well as before it?

13. Discuss Holden's literary tastes.

14. The structure of the novel indicates that Holden is telling the story of these four days considerably later, in California, to an analyst. What is his attitude to the earlier Holden, the

one who was the actor, "last Christmas," in the re-counted events?

15. Why does Holden, obviously an educated, literate person who does *NOT* wish to be associated with the "phonies" at school, take such pains to speak the dialect he uses?

16. To what extent is Salinger's life reflected in his fiction?

Your Guides to Successful Test Preparation.

Cliffs Test Preparation Guides

Efficient preparation means better test scores. Go with the experts and use **Cliffs Test Preparation Guides**. They'll help you reach your goals because they're: • Complete • Concise • Functional • In-depth. They are focused on helping you know what to expect from each test. The test-taking techniques have been proven in classroom programs nationwide.

Recommended for individual use or as a part of formal test preparation programs.

Available at your local bookseller or order by sending the coupon with your check.

Cliffs Notes, P.O. Box 80728, Lincoln, NE 68501

	TITLES	QTY.
2004-1	ACT ($4.95)	
2030-0	CBEST ($6.95)	
1471-8	ESSAY EXAM ($2.95)	
2016-5	GED Mathematics ($3.95)	
2014-9	GED Reading Skills ($2.95)	
2010-6	GED Science ($3.95)	
2012-2	GED Social Studies ($3.95)	
2015-7	GED Writing Skills ($3.95)	
2006-8	GMAT ($5.95)	
2008-4	GRE ($5.95)	
2021-1	LSAT ($5.95)	
2017-3	NTE ($9.95)	
2002-5	PSAT/NMSQT ($3.25)	
2000-9	SAT ($4.95)	
2018-1	TOEFL ($14.95)	

Name_____

Address_____

City_____

State _____ Zip_____

Cliffs NOTES INC.

P.O. Box 80728
Lincoln, NE 68501

Prices subject to change without notice.

Do You Know Someone Special?

Cliffs Speech and Hearing Series can help with many special education problems

This series of up-to-date overviews helps you quickly become familiar with areas of special education. As a student, teacher or concerned individual, these easy-to-follow presentations also give you helpful definition of terms, glossary and an annotated bibliography.

ORDER BLANK

		QTY.
1816-0	Aphasia ($3.95)	
1810-1	Articulation Disorders; Methods of Evaluation and Therapy ($3.95)	
1830-6	Auditory Processing and Learning Disabilities ($3.95)	
1813-6	Basic Audiometry — Including Impedance Measurement ($2.75)	
1819-5	Cerebral Palsy: Speech, Hearing, and Language Problems ($3.95)	
1801-2	Cleft Palate and Associated Speech Characteristics ($3.95)	
1803-9	Clinical Management of Voice Disorders ($3.95)	
1826-8	Hearing Impairment Among Aging Persons ($2.75)	
1832-2	Language Disorders in Adolescents	
1828-4	Speech-Hearing Pathology and Surgery ($4.95)	
1807-1	Speech and Hearing Problems in the Classroom ($3.95)	
1805-5	Stuttering: What It Is and What To Do About It ($3.95)	
1822-5	Tongue Thrust ($3.95)	

Name _____

Address _____

City _____

State _____ Zip _____

P.O. Box 80728
Lincoln, NE 68501

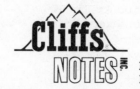